Walt Disney's MICKEY AND FRIENDS
LET'S GO
to the Fire Station

By Lucy Geist

Illustrated by DiCicco Digital Arts

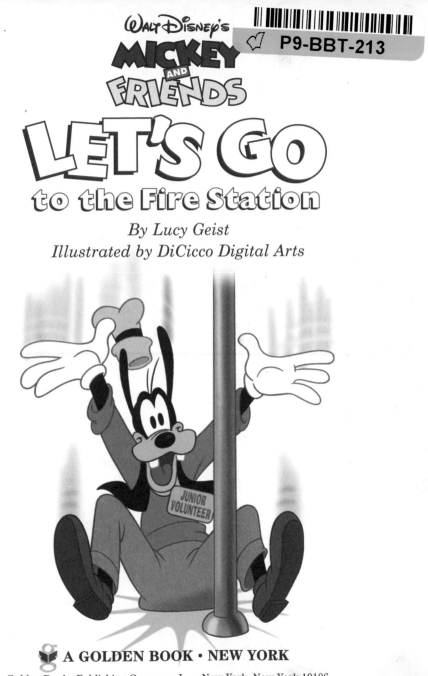

JUNIOR VOLUNTEER

A GOLDEN BOOK · NEW YORK

Golden Books Publishing Company, Inc., New York, New York 10106

Let's paint racing stripes on the old engine!" Huey exclaimed.

Mickey Mouse laughed. "Hold it!" he said. "We still want it to look like a fire truck." Mickey and the boys were on their way to the fire station. They had offered to decorate an antique fire engine for the Town Day parade the next day.

"Uncle Donald is working on a top-secret parade float," said
Louie. "He won't let us see it."

"Don't worry," Mickey answered. "Our fine old engine will
be the pride of the parade."

Mickey and the others arrived just in time to see their friend Goofy slide down the brass pole in the middle of the fire station.

"Hi-ya, gang," said Goofy.

"Goofy is a junior volunteer, just like me," Mickey told the boys, as he leaned over to pat a friendly Dalmatian. "This is Freckles, the fire station's mascot."

"Here's our parade engine." Goofy grinned as he led the
boys to an old-fashioned pumper truck. "Isn't she a beauty?"
Mickey started polishing the engine while Goofy and the
boys went to work on the decorations.

"Does this truck still work?" asked one of the boys.
Mickey nodded. "Yes, it works, but it's not as fast or as
powerful as the newer engines. Now we just use it
for parades."

After a while, Mickey and the others walked over to look at the shiny, modern fire engines.

"So this is the hook and ladder," said Goofy. "Of course, the one behind it is the pumper truck."

"Goofy, you have it backward!" said Mickey. "*This* is the pumper truck. Boys, it has a powerful pump in it—to force the water through the hoses."

"It must be hard work being a firefighter," Louie said.

"It sure is," Goofy responded proudly. "Do you remember when the big hotel caught fire? We had to rescue about twenty people. I even saved Mrs. Porter's parakeet."

"Gosh, Goofy," said Mickey. "If I remember right, the regular firefighters rescued the parakeet. They just gave it to you to hold."

"But I was a big help," Goofy insisted. "I went and found Mrs. Porter and gave her back her bird."

Then Goofy changed the subject.

"I'll tell you another story, boys," he said. "A couple of years ago, there was a big fire in the park outside town."

"What happened?" the boys asked eagerly.

"A campfire roared out of control," said Goofy. "But I rushed boldly into the forest. That night we saved the woods from being burned to the ground."

"I remember that night," said Mickey. "It was cold. You and I passed blankets out to the campers. I don't remember doing much else."

Goofy looked embarrassed. After that, he didn't tell any
more stories. He and the others finally finished decorating the
engine and headed home together. Everybody looked forward
to the next day—the day of the big parade.

The following day, the whole town turned out to watch the parade. The antique truck led the way—with Mickey at the wheel. The boys were allowed to ride in the back with Goofy.

"We're going to win the blue ribbon for best parade entry," said Huey. He looked back over his shoulder. "Uncle Donald's float doesn't have a chance."

Donald's float was just behind the fire engine. He had mounted a spaceship on his old pickup truck.

"Hey, Donald!" someone called from the crowd. "Is that a real rocket ship?"

"Almost," Donald answered proudly. "Get a good look. My float is going to send the judges to the moon."

Donald drove his wobbly rocket on down the street, sparks flying everywhere.

Suddenly the rocket caught fire. Within seconds, the whole float was in flames.

"Help!" squawked Donald. "Fire!"

"I'll save you!" Goofy cried. As Mickey pulled to a stop, Goofy jumped off the fire truck. He grabbed one of the old engine's hoses and hooked it to a nearby hydrant. Then Goofy began spraying Donald's float with water. Before long, the fire was completely out.

Goofy was a hero at last. During the award ceremony after
the parade, the mayor asked him to come forward.

"Goofy, I'd like you to accept this blue ribbon with our
thanks," said the mayor. "You were very brave today. In fact,
you're the bravest junior volunteer who ever held a hose!"